Reverie

Jomayra Y. J.

BookLeaf
Publishing

India | USA | UK

Presentation by *BookLeaf Publishing*

Web: www.bookleafpub.com

E-mail: info@bookleafpub.com

ISBN: 9789357445856

First edition 2022

DEDICATION

To my mother,

for making everything possible and within my grasp. You push me to keep moving forward whenever I was ready to give up.

To my great grandfather,

I never got to truly meet you, but you were the most interesting person I was fortunate enough to have in my life.

To my loved ones,

all of you drive me crazy, but hank you for reminding me every day love and support in those times of need.

To you,

for picking this book out of many more. You, the wonderful reader, are amazing. Stay starry.

/petunias/

even as these words come to my mind,
once lingering thoughts transforming into
phrases of ink,
you peek through the corners of its pages,
and a part of me wishes that you will read them
in realizing what you have left behind,
perhaps it is selfish of me,
to force myself push past this pain in my heart,
but i have tire of mourning a missing person

i want to look at a picture of my family,
  without wondering who you were,
enjoy spending time with her,
  without the remembrance of when you left us,
i want to smile for my sister when she dances
with him,
  without ever dreaming of what it would be with
you,
even as i spend my important moments,
you are there, peeking at the corner

you are not completely gone, i fear you never
will,
but this child you left long ago still hopes you
stay,

despite whatever i try to convince myself all
these years,
a part of me wishes you will find me again,
even if i grow older where my hair shines in
silver,
even if i have to shiver under a thundering
storm,
i will stay dreaming of you.

/flannel flower/

the bark of my skin scratches your palms
my yellow leaves softly land on your face
 roots burrowing deep within the rocks
you lean against my trunk,
 safety easily provided as my branches sink
like blankets, hiding you from the burning sun

i open my eyes to see the looming buildings
 so many pairs of shoes rushing to and fro
i hide in the corner of the world
 warm hues dressing my empty branches
you see for me for a second
before being one of the many

/yellow tulips/

plucking flowers felt childish,
 these petals switching from one to two,
all for a feeling in my heart,
   a flutter in my stomach,
waiting felt more reasonable,
 becoming friends felt safer than picking flowers
i don't want something small
 like a simple petal
to be my final judgement nor
 be a hope that pushes this crush further,
but when the results came from its last,
 i plucked another from my heart

/narcissus/

beautiful brown locks of hair,
soft and dainty,
sitting on her shoulders,
strawberry-scented,
weaving fingers through her hair,
she leans back on the grass,
squeezing the soil between her toes

her lips of cherry and rose,
eyes made of nature's grass, gold, and bark
the trees bend when she gazes at their beauty,
words breaking and transforming the world
into a perspective twisted or stretched,
lies white as daises,
but an honest mirror

she smiles so kindly,
nails sharp and ready to strike,
the ground shakes at her very steps,
her mind creating stories so glorious,
she is beautiful,
even if her head says anything else.

/garden balsam/

swaying my body to this electrifying beat,
i can no longer stay in my seat,
the piano keys and guitar strum,
moving to my own drum,
sliding across the ground,
dancing to this heart-thrilling sound,
my hand flies to your shoulders, gripping tightly,
you throw me in the air, smiling so brightly,
this night is barely beginning,
how much i love this evening,
knee high dress with kitten heels,
bright red cars with white-rimmed wheels,
baby, you got me longing,
for a dance worth swinging

/iris/

in the southern fields of grass,
life vividly existed in nature's hues
northern streets were crowded yet friendly,
and the west's cities shined like stars
when those trees of oak turned to cedar,
the breeze became sweeter
rivers appeared along the roads,
and things blurred right past
an endless path forward,
fireflies among the canopy of leaves,
sand sneaking into the sandals
only to end back
in the same old empty room.

/hellebore/

this uneasiness replaces the oxygen,
settling itself deep into my lungs,
it weighs my heart with this dread,
pulling down towards my stomach,
fogging up my skull,
and soon, from somewhere deep within,
it releases into a self-made smog,
repeating the cycle

/coreopsis/

she stops and smiles at the snails
soft adoration in their trails
when everyone pushes right past
she hopes these little minutes last
the leaves of pink flowers
weather grey of its showers
his hair frizzy and skin cold
hands out to hold
cracks in the cement
their smiles so content

when i lean on my arm,
watching them from a see-through wall,
hoping one day i can be,
a snail that small.

/yarrow/

to be hero of a story
brings sorrow to such a feeble heart,
but if given the chance
to be the world's ends of destruction,
brings lightness in this miserable disgrace of a
person.
it's almost hilarious to see how happy one would
be
to be a hero of a story

/rue/

wretchedness of a poor human,
pulled apart by a machine,
the body tugged and then ripped off,
metal crumbled like nothing,
paper ripped by simple hands,
what a wrecked state of despicable morality,
this yearning to be watched,
at the cost of tortured humanity

/oleander/

I have known I mattered to you
like a crumb on a plate,
My existence was just another voice
I trust what movies have promised me,
Of your love towards me
When your actions stated otherwise,
Your honeyed words and smiles
What once brought joy,
Now makes me sickly disgusted
We never became more,
Reasoning kept me sane
You knew my vulnerability to you,
The way I lightened the tone of my voice
Whispering secrets of heart,
I sit outside under a lamp post,
Waiting for a dream I so foolishly believed in

/borage flowers/

for the way you grow,
proudness in your achievements,
once hate, now new love

/lupine/

i was looking for romance in an empty road,
waiting for it with my thumb raised up,
shamelessly hoping for someone to stop for me,
so if it finally came, i was ready to love
somebody other than myself
because in this barren path of once was,
i thought that someone finally wanted to love
me.

/mandrake/

as i peer over the edge of my cobblestone tower,
  i see you shouting words, desperately trying to climb
like a frustrated child,
  you demand me to kneel and listen

it is utterly pathetic
the way your lips pucker and arms crossed,
how you try to command my absolute loyalty
when you yourself amount to the pebble in my
cobblestone tower

i watch until the moon arises from the trees,
  you, a foolish child, still screaming
when i closed the window of this looming tower,
  for a second, you pause before yelling once
more

/red camellia/

we may not have started everything together,
  but when I moved those heavy boxes,
you stepped up instantly to help me.
our conversations move seamlessly,
  bouncing from the erratic weather
to admitting our deepest feelings of others.
we lean on each other,
  my cold feet planted on your stomach
 as you try to push me away,
only to encouraging me to stick like skin on hot
leather
  if you allow me back to the kitchen,
 i would cook you the grandest meal from my
simple gift;
soft mashed potatoes with melting butter and
cheese;
  scrambled eggs combined with vegetables to
add into the rice;
 stuffed chicken with broccoli and cheese.
my wonderous sun, the world has so much in
plan for us.

/oenothera/

i stand in a room full of cacti,
 pricking my skin with vivd, eye-catching
flowers
there is barely anything alive under this burning
light,
 my throat aching to drink,
i thought shoveling the sand at my feet,
 but i continued to stand
at times, i hear whispers of an oasis not too far
North,
 but it dried itself, a myth long forgotten
i motivate myself to stay for a few more
minutes,
 counting the tumbleweeds or the cracks in the
soil
yet in this desert,
 i find myself gazing at the clouds.

/sunflower's heart/

i don't believe i could love you;
despite, how much i try to convince myself
i can not passionately adorn you in wares nor in
loving words,
what i offer is practically a bowl of rice
while others could offer heaps of gold and gems,
though with that bowl,
i could make you food
while they struggle to keep you alive.

/jonquil/

an uncontrollable hopelessness hits me
the moment i am in a group of people
i want to be under this thin string of light for a
brief blink of an eye,
have others, for once, look at who i am and what
i offer in love.
i want people to actually see me, listen to my
jumbled words,
and just continue to listen.
i don't need someone to talk my problems out,
nor do i want someone to take matters in their
own hands,
i want them to just pull me in their arms,
holding me just as tightly,
and listening to the thoughts bursting out of a
spun soda bottle.
Just hug me.

/larkspur/

like a walnut, you cracked under the pressure of
the one with many eyes,
but when i saw you, you were a beautiful gem.

/pink carnations & cherry blossoms/

My love for you, goes beyond hills and where
the sea devours
You wait for me under a sanctuary full of
flowers

Good morning dew lands on the leaves of your
avocado tree,
Lassoed into a dance of spinning twisters on the
dance floor,
Only you can make the time freeze with pure
stubbornness,
Right before we jump, you were already with the
birds soaring,
I hesitate too often, fearful of the wrong,
Oblivious to my discomfort, you push me
forward to fly
Under the million stars in this everlasting sky,
Sometimes, you were the only one who actually
believed in me

Many birthdays will come with a cake split for
you and I,

Observing the way you change that once empty
wall of pictures into
The most beautiful tree in our house
However, these years start and end,
Everything may change in what we see or learn,
Remember mom, you are always my number
one.

/lily of the valley/

i am patient in the way i wait for the darkness to
fully set in, before closing my blinds; pick up
the plates when everyone has finished; listen
when everyone has long walked off; stay for the
chance of ever meeting someone again.

but that does not mean i will not leave.

i am a tree who bears your fruit of the day,
the river in which fish can play,
an echo of the cave to offer company,
i am whatever you need me to be,
but i am not someone who forgets to step away.

don't ever take my kindness as obedience.
my kindness is strength and love for you,
 do not taint it with your selfish actions.